ANIMALS OF THE SAHARA

Wildlife of the Desert Encyclopedias for Children

Speedy Publishing LLC
40 E. Main St. #1156
Newark, DE 19711
www.speedypublishing.com

The Sahara is the largest hot desert in the world.

The olive baboon is named for its coat, which, at a distance, is a shade of green-grey.

The Anubis baboon survives well because of its diversified diet, which includes plants, birds, and even small mammals.

The dama gazelle is white with a tannish-brown head and neck. Dama gazelles eat shrubs, succulents, herbs, trees, and woody plants.

Damas are considered the largest type of gazelle. Dama Gazelle is active during the daytime.

The jerboa is a member of the rodent family. Jerboa lives in underground burrows.

Jerboa usually leaps distance of 5 inches, but when it needs to escape from predators, jerboa can jump distance of 9.8 feet.

Spotted hyenas are large, dog-like, carnivores. Spotted hyenas can reach 35 inches in height and 90 pounds in weight.

Spotted hyenas live in large groups called clans, which can include up to 80 hyenas.

Secretary bird can reach 4 to 5 feet in height and 5 to 9 pounds of weight. Couples work together to build huge nests high in acacia trees.

Secretary
birds are
carnivores.
Their diet
consists of
snakes and
other reptiles,
insects and
rodents.

The dromedary camel is a single humped camel. Dromedaries usually reach a little over 7 feet tall, including the hump.

Dromedary camels weigh 300 to 600 kg. The humps contain fatty tissue reserves, which can be converted to water or energy when required.

Ostriches are the largest bird in the world. They can grow up to 9 feet tall and weigh up to 350 pounds.

Ostriches have powerful legs and clawed toes. One strong kick can kill a lion.

The
Deathstalker
Scorpion is
about 4 inches
in size for the
females and
the males are
about 3 inches.

The
deathstalker
is regarded
as the most
dangerous
species of
scorpion.
Its venom is
a powerful
mixture of
neurotoxins.

The fennec fox is the smallest member of the dog family. The coats of fennec foxes are very pale, helping them reflect most of the sunlight that falls on them.

Its most distinctive feature is its unusually large ears, which also serve to dissipate heat.

Visit

BABY PROFESSOR
EDUCATION KIDS

www.BabyProfessorBooks.com
to download Free Baby Professor eBooks
and view our catalog of new and exciting
Children's Books